SUNBURST

Raymond Tallis

Poems

IRON
PRESS

First published 2019 by IRON Press
5 Marden Terrace
Cullercoats
North Shields
NE30 4PD
tel +44(0)191 2531901
ironpress@xlnmail.com
www.ironpress.co.uk

ISBN 978-1-9997636-3-3
Printed by Imprint Digital

Cover and book design Brian Grogan and Peter Mortimer

Typeset in Georgia 9pt
Image Photography by Barry McCulloch
Sunlight through a stained glass window in Manchester Cathedral

IRON Press books are distributed by
NBN International
and represented by Inpress Ltd
Milburn House, Dean Street
Newcastle upon Tyne NE1 1LF
tel: +44(0)191 2308104
www.inpressbooks.co.uk

Supported using public funding by
ARTS COUNCIL ENGLAND
LOTTERY FUNDED

SUNBURST

Tallis on Tallis

I HAVE BEEN WRITING ALMOST DAILY FOR NEARLY HALF A CENTURY. WHILE MY forty or so published volumes have encompassed philosophical treatises, poetry, essays on every subject under the sun, literary criticism, fiction, and medicine, poetry and philosophy have been my most long-standing preoccupations. The present collection includes a poem I wrote in my teens, that has been endlessly revised in subsequent decades. For me poetry and philosophy have fundamentally the same aim: to connect the small details that detain us with the great facts that enclose us.

The great poet Paul Valéry tried to capture the distinctive virtue of poetry when he said that – courtesy of features such as rhyme and rhythm – a poem 'hesitates between sound and sense'. And then there are metaphors that jolt us out of our customary ways of thinking and unpeel the patina that routines deposit on our gaze. By these and other means, poetry foregrounds language, thereby celebrating the ocean of connected meaning in which we swim absent-mindedly, whose depths are lost in the busyness of everyday life.

The novelist André Gide once said that he wrote to be *re*-read. This does not seem an impossible demand for a form marked by brevity. A poem can be read at a sitting and re-read endlessly, allowing different senses to be unpacked and different pleasures experienced. It can be committed to memory, making it available to be recalled in solitude.

There are poems that have accompanied me throughout my life, when I have been called out for the hundredth time in a busy weekend on duty, or rocking a pram, or back-packing in the hills. They have linked the different seasons of my life. On 21st December every year since 1970, I have recited John Donne's *A Nocturnal Upon St. Lucy's Day* and each time discovered something new.

In an increasingly hurried world, where we scamper from place to place, task to task, tweet to tweet, email to email, poetry says: 'Stop', 'Look', 'Listen', 'Imagine', 'Think'. The way the poem is laid out on the page, the silence in which it is framed - signified by the width of its margins and the generous spaces between lines and verses - solicits special attention. There is presumption in such a demand and the poem has to earn what it asks of the reader. Poets with a conscience will have destroyed many more poems or versions of poems than they will offer to readers. The reader will judge whether the poems in this collection deserve the attention they seek.

Raymond Tallis

Raymond Tallis

Raymond Tallis is a retired physician and clinical neuroscientist. He ran a large clinical service in Hope Hospital Salford and an academic department in the University of Manchester. His research focused on epilepsy, stroke, and neurological rehabilitation. He has 4 honorary degrees: DLitt (Hull, 1997) and Litt.D. (Manchester, 2001) for contributions to the humanities; and DSc (St George's Hospital Medical School, 2015; University of East Anglia, 2017) for contributions to research in medicine.

He has published fiction, poetry, and 25 books on the philosophy of mind, philosophical anthropology, literary and cultural criticism. Sunburst is his fourth volume of verse.

In 2009, the Economist Intelligent Life Magazine described him as one of the world's leading polymaths.

The Poems

Sunburst

Sunburst surprises the saint-stained glass.
The glory of the apostles is recharged
with grace borrowed from the radiance
that dazzles Easter shoppers in the Mall.

Between umbra and penumbra, beneath
flying buttresses of light, the churched
sing towards transcendence. The chiaroscuro
of the moment is a painted dream.

Its radiance recalls childhood, awakens
whatever sense remains of holiness, in light
and dark. Lithographic memories,
pasts whose glimmers are depths in us.

Forgotten classrooms stir: history guiding
memory to places before itself, disclosing
the fathoms on which we float.
We are embarked. Whither, who knows?

QUATTRO STAGIONE

Bluebells

From a distance, scarves of mist, whiffs of smoke.
Closer, irregulars picnicking in the lengthening grass
that quilts the tree-shaded slope of the meadow.

Drooped by foreknowledge of transience,
their heads summarise
hues of memory and distance,

nod to an openness where sounds,
framed by cubic leagues of silence,
are changed to the possibility of music.

Letters to the Idea of Summer Evenings

(1)
Evening, your light makes such love
to all things that all things,
in your light, are easier to love.
Your longueurs - obliquities of sunlight,
Giacometti shadows - smooth the ripples
and the wrinkles in the fabric of the day,
evening the odds and oddities of time.

(2)
Towards dusk a slight headache
is a congested song:
too many compacted notes,
pressing to be unravelled
in a thrush's throat to an aria
that fills the fenceless heights
threshed by the tallest trees,
with an unthrobbing coolness,
evening's own evensong.

(3)
Though yours are the hours when daylight's breath
thickens to stifled night, and sickness to the sick
becomes the standing truth of things,
a one-way tunnel from the world, as windows
change to mirrors gazing inward
into rooms transformed to bathyspheres;

yours the sickened minutes sick when children hear
their heartbeats as gouts of blood,
and footsteps eat the distance on the stair;
when bewitched, bewildered, the driver,
squinting between light and twilight,
resolves your ambiguities in a fatal smack;
and yours the shadows that shepherd cruelty
inwards from the street,
hidden from the judgement of the just...

Yes, all of this, and yet
still shall I love you, evening, since
your breezes silk the softness of the leaves,
their woken voices massage jagged thought,
and your roads and streets, deepen,
to tree-lined *avenidas* linking
honeyed combs of ingled inskirts,
and brickwork is softened with tiredness,
mossed with human time, and pavements
return intact the kindness of our care.

(4)
After the bright arterial mornings
and the weary venous blood of afternoons,
the world is an earful of murmurs,
homeward traffic rumours of another shore,

as if the summed-up day were a wave
breaking on a space as wide as time.

Near-hush strains for silence,
inviting the organ roar of fact
to pause, and us to listen
into glades allowing pianissimo notes:
the seedlings of Perhaps,
the intact foam of Possibility.

(5)
The greatness of the evening
is to care for little things:
hopes the size of nests, worlds
scoped by candlelight, the toy behind
the chair, laughter in the cot,
the hand on the shoulder, frail words,
glances gleaming in the gloom.

The greatness of the evening
is its boundlessness.
Laughter mocked by a barn owl's call
sounds the vastness of a valley
between the hills; articulates the space
between the crags and the stars;
between those stars and yet more stars.

October Song

Time has reached its occident, the yellow world is sick:
occultation of the sunlight, darkening of the land.
Smoke, a seasoned mist, processes into space
from pyres of time-wrecked Summer cremated in the dusk.

October, flanked by embers, ignites amid decay
a candle-dim candescence of ochre in the gloom,
milliwatts of brightness from megawatts of sun
leaves that fade to tawdry litter, marking Summerset.

It's over, yes, it's over, grins the jaundice of October...
and the death-gold afternoon is night-tinged octoroon*
as the year declines through evening and the ripeness
splits to rot.

The sick, the old, the loners hear their howling in the air
voiced on wind-played ocarinas, mourning in the dark
beloved light's engulfment by the octopus of night.

* *An archaic term used originally to refer to a person
who was one eighth black by descent.*

Decembrance

A clear, cold windless dawn
enlightens sherbet tiles,
candied webs on webs of twigs,
candid fields of grass and fallen leaves.

Smoke's seamless growth conjures
fat squirrel tails unpacked from sullen wood,
cross-referencing in the still air
the stock dove's fluffed up grey asides.

Someone has lit a fire to unpack time
from the stasis of a world where burgeoning and rot
are both on pause. Flames undo
the Summer's logged alluvium
compiled from stifling afternoons when
leaf-sipped light married leaf-inspired air.

How brief it was, how brief!

MODES OF SLEEP

Fixed

*'...moved by an overwhelming
love for all mankind...'*

Love enters through the arm,
veins it to the hungry brain.
Released from the windowless interior,
 from the unforgiving time-table of his need,
he is uncoupled from his body and from the streets
that held him down as blotters fasten ink.

Soars.
Sprouting one Left and one half-broken wing,
hero unites with heroin and prophesies:
horse and flying rider castigate
a corrupt, untuned quotidian world.

Time slackens to trance,
trance purples to joy
life bathes in a glow of memory...
A smile as wide as evening steals across the hour,
nurses the waning day in a solvent calm
so composed in its stillness
the slightest act would bruise its sky.

Thus is love complete.
He need not stir one poppy-heavy head
to help the howling, wretches of a world
exiled to the tuneless grey
outside the singing rainbows of his dream....

Till the brain-wolves wake again
baying for their intravenous love

Ashburial

The day was gloves
John Ashbery

The curtain's vertical frown
and the settee's complicity
steward our meanings. Thus
are we spared the suck of absence
in the foamless wake of one who wakes not.

We are (still) here and it is (very) ordinary.
The fridge shudders, suffering
our chill, validating our concerns.

Duty Free

Über allen Gipfeln ist Ruh*
Goethe

The Alps are behind us. Double-triplexed
against the rage of space
and the agonising search
for oxygen and warmth, we overflew
their snow-dusted peaks and bivouacs of rock.

Ten thousand feet and descending towards Zurich
our steady motion seems a stillness,
deceptive as the the orbiting of the Earth.
From here (between a seminar and its slides,
next to a glass of wine translating
flight into standing circles),
the tall-grassed Spring-time meadows
are Swiss-tidy: insectless, and shaved to baize.

The sounds of aphids on the autobahn,
of the laughter in the streets,
and the baby crying in the darkened room
are quenched by remoteness.
The heft and fluff of things
is cancelled to weightless smooth.

Our descent steepens.
'Free fall' segues to 'let down'.
The undercarriage clunk,
foretold in the folding of the folding tables.
The slam of lockers overhead,

prepares us to relinquish our vantage point.
The Airbus closes on its fattening shadow,
once a distant mark on clouds and fields.
Hedges, houses, nearing, report its *rallentando* **
as headlong flight.

Fat-tyred jouncing
Astonished engines suck back the haste
that had transformed air into airlift.
The pricked-up wings - Pluto's startled ears
as he slithers, friction-pawed to a halt –
stir turbulence, viscosity, and brakes into the air.

At stand.
The world resumes its weight.
Your baggage reclaims you:
Possessions re-possess possessors,
luggage to be lugged.
Your name and title chalked on cardboard held aloft:
'The University of X welcomes Professor Y'.
End of weightlessness.
The burr returns to its Velcro cage.
No longer duty free.

* *Above all the summits it is calm.*
** *A term referring to slowing down of the music.*

Latecomers

A complaint in carpet slippers

Our thinkers don't have visions any more.
We've had our fill of prophets and their like:
apocalyptic quill-men earn our scorn.
Curricula entomb The Big Ideas,
less 'True' or 'False' than 'Fragments of the Past'.
This is the age of critics, queries, notes,
of satirists, allusion, meta-minds.
No master-brain incises light on dark.

We'll die, of course, like those who thought they thought,
but *we'll* be quite relaxed when darkness comes,
still smiling at those loons who found life strange:
their questioning a trifle over-wrought,
as if the sense of things were incomplete.

Notes Towards a Definition
of Mr. Eliot

He suffered (as the super-cultivated must)
an intricate and erudite despair.
Bore wearily, with irony, obliquities of grief,
imperfect pains whose maps were yet undrawn.

Tendrils reaching down from besuited days
siphoned Mr. Prufrock's pinstriped scream.
Elaborated echoes of that cry,
adorned it with the ruins of 'The West':
defunct collective certainties that
Time had spat from History to Wednesdays at the bank.

Assumed in youth the voice of gummy age:
obtuse Polonius piping shrilly round his doom;
gynaecoid Tiresias; Gerontion -
ruminating at eventide; Oedipus at Colonus,
broken pensioners of slender means.

Propriety and emptiness walked
side by side in handcuffs on the beach,
dazzled in the wordless open air,
sickened by demotic pleasure pits
the drunkard's dream, witless vulgarity,
the sty-work and the slobber-joys of lust.

II

The void within began to sense an edge,
assumed a shape that fitted certain words.
His sharp-toothed lack was de Nerval's 'empty sky',
the ache of Absence proof of hidden Presence.

The new-found God approved the coldness in his thoughts,
His Church admired those passionate distastes.
Hunger walked the aisle with solemn creeds
that housed the tangled places of his heart,
combed the unkempt watches of the night.

The acentric light of pain, the raving voice,
modulated into quiet music of the mind,
the flame of grief dressed itself
in sober talk, bespectacled and tired.

The end: infertile peace, an after-dinner sleep,
happiness no Prufrock could conceive.

Shades of Grey

The poplars by the silvered railway tracks
are still as bronze this hollow moonlit hour.
Autumn had pruned their vocal leaves, untongued
the sounds
that lately fretted open-windowed nights
and goosed the pools of shallow, sweaty sleep.

Only rags of ghosts trouble Auntie's haunted house -
dream-moths zigging and zagging from
the ruined brocade and broken springs of years -
set free by the permissiveness of sleep.
These – and soliloquies of the fridge,
and the monosyllabic dripping of the tap
and the gas fire's unremitting sigh -
define her world until the time-tabled catastrophe
of the late, late train violates
stillness with murderous haste.

Auntie wakes into grammarless wondering,
wanders disused lanes of thought, moved
by time-bleached wants and old concerns,
leftovers, cuttings from forgotten summers.

Bent on nothing, bent on being bent,
she zimmers her ninety years to the open door.
Night-gowned in the street,
brailles past autistic streetlamps towards
imaginary shopping hours in memory stores
deregulated as her mind.

Purposive without purpose;
unsure, like me, where to find
a final sense in things.

PARENTAL ANNOTATIONS

Overdue

For L.J.T.

Has someone started growing
towards our world,
moving eyeless through the dark
towards the light
from nowhere to our place in space and time?

A speechless patience
learning to unpack
no-one's silence into someone's speech,
travelling from conception to conceptions
shared with us?

A secret - setting off
towards our days,
towards a future life,
At home in ours?

Fallen Newborn

Time was never his to use or waste.
It never left the flutter of his pulse
to cool in clocks or – portioned, numbered, tamed –
returned to perch, his servant, on his wrist.
He never owned his hours, caged tabled days
or mapped them into futures of his own.
He was Time's possession, Time that broke him up
and dispossessed him of his nascent world.

Knew ceaseless care but not who gave the care.
The uniforms who tended him in shifts
were nameless as the forms outside the glass
who kept the shiftless vigil of their grief.
No friends. Nor enemies – he needed none:
his body was at total war with change.
And knew no fear. There was no space for fear
since he could not conceive a worse than Now.

The little ungrowing parcel of his flesh
(his hands remote to him as distant stars)
maintained a course tangential to the world
that missed the weave of voices, lights and shades,
of days he did not learn to occupy.

The glimmer in his body's turbid toil
grew dim inside the gathering helplessness
and, somewhere in the unmapped dark, went out.

Infans

For B.C.T.

*Little of our mind dwells in our natural body; a truly human intellect
dwells in us only when our lips shape words and our eyes read print.*
Michael Polanyi

Pip of nascent self. Attention is
directed eyes and reaching limbs,
focussing of body, not of thought.
Mouth fastens to the breast
like a barnacle to a rock.
Not in his mind
but in his gut he ruminates:
no yeast of words allows
solitary need to swell
to open utterance; cavitate
to inward, secret places of reserve;
or find their image and perfection
in the spacious empires of the printed world.

Senses hold him down to what he is
and what he is is what they say he is.
Tomorrow cannot mitigate today:
this moment cannot borrow distant sense
from past and future; for they demand
names and verbs to pluck them from the void.

That's why his mirth chuckles deep
beneath the deepest reach of wit;
why his sorrow's salt stings sharper
than the bitterest tang of speech.

Three Years Old

For L.J.T.

Our world
through his eyes.
Stale old world-light
refracted through dew.

SPEECH ACTS

Cries

Become a frightful thing of darkness
to frighten away the dark

Darkness is spiked with a thousand cries:
imagined or real, jungle or cot;
gin-trapped paw or broken heart;
edge-of-world piping,
scimitar-slits in the estuarine
silence of evening silting from the east;
or sleep-murdering shouts blotting
the fuddled noctuary of the eventide home.

So many cries in so much dark
because sadness must hear itself,
grief find salving remoteness,
sorrow bathe in square miles of nowhere,
triangulated by elsewheres where groans
weaken from heard to overheard,
recruiting rings of sympathy and fear.

With quill pen or larynx, mews or muse,
with cursors chasing curses in moon-chrome pixels,
with sky-raking bellows excavating emptiness -

thus do the possessed of the earth
possess the earth.

The Gospel According to St. John Chapter 1, Verse 14 (a)

The public's pains vex no-one, Sam Johnson said,
touching on our utter fallenness.
See how we supp'd on horrors Sunday night:
The Mafia first, then on to Ravensbruck.
At midnight, we repaired to dreamless sleep
and woke a.m. refreshed to go to work
and chat about the death camps over lunch.

The Critic's mind, more finely tuned than ours,
found Sunday's telly murdered Sunday's sleep.
His keyboard tapping kept the kids awake,
the software weaving drafts of his lament.

He earns his keep by feeling things in print;
so went to bed in peace on Monday night,
his weekly column-inches in the bag.
'That final image...' (infant-fattened flames)
had 'haunted' him; so Flesh returned to Word

Away Match

He winked across at her again; she liked his foreign cheek -
the 'he' a handsome Marseillais, the 'she' a pretty Greek.
Each sensed in each a mystery that part of each did seek,
though neither could (bar "Yes" and "No") the other's/
                               language speak.

Their minds convened in English words, their chat up/
                               dressed in sounds
acquired in language classes steeped in boredom, sighs/
                               and frowns.
The lonely place of exile turned to flower-strewn/
                               common grounds
as mental francs and drachmas were exchanged/
                               for pence and pounds.

They saved each other's native tongues for teasing/
                               and for play:
"*Bonjour m'sieur*" she ironized as she met his smile/
                               each day;
"*Kali nikta*" he would murmur as at night he went away.
Thus native tongue touched foreign tongue till tongue/
                               on tongue they lay.

Soon English was a hindrance as their hearts began/
                               to race.
Their friendship moved to places where the schoolroom/
                               had no place.
Its stilted phrases limped behind their pulses'/
                               quickening pace,

and pedagogues and syntax mocked their/
                    awkwardness and grace.

At the climax in the darkness, it was French and/
                    Greek again -
at the apex of their loving where his love began to end.

He boasted in the morning of her "*mamelles*" to his friend.
She wrote her anxious letters with her close Hellenic pen.

The English of the textbook seemed inadequate and trite,
to deal with his evasions when she told him of her plight.
His charm was bricked in anger on that dreadful/
                    tongueless night
when, fresh from her abortion, she provoked his/
                    coward flight.

A man resides in Southern France who has, for many years,
avoided certain English words: they carry guilt he fears.
A woman lives in Thessaly whom English moves to tears,
adopted tongue that mocked her love when smiles/
                    gave way to jeers.

THE OWL OF MINERVA

Concrete Poem

The real Outside has neither memory nor history:
the heel's hard clop receives a clipped reply.
No inner echoes smudge its stencilled vacancy
where neither sweat collects nor sorrow recollects.
Silence before, amnesia after, dissect events:
crisply shod bodies tap the street's sharp crust.
Voices die into the unrecording chamber of the night:
each where is anywhere and forgets an idle shout,
a scuttering that continues a while and then stops,
someone whistling a wire of sound snipped by a door
snapped snugly shut, shards of noise hinged by silences,
a boundless cold lidlessly surveyed by the
Polyphemus-blind, glaucous eyeball of the night.
But look! Twitched by window glass, the moon
wobbles amoeboid. Beyond the glass, its chlorinated
light slants inwards into darkness to touch the places
where grease can cling and scents and warmth take root
and Space and Time are the warp and weft of days,
days that carry names and incise their passage on faces
as they seep into the mind, those places
where memory and history live - the real Inside.

Edges

A falcon's urgent solitude draws a new horizon:
his far and high pass judgement on our low domestic spaces.
Limits, viewed from afar, promise new permissions.

Down below, like burrs in a mesh of tabled time,
caught in the marshes and sunless canyons
of unquestioned ought, something in us reaches
for the unwritten, to shuffle all the meanings time
has weathered into the unarresting look of things,
imprisoned in rasping flatness of the voice.

Vanishing into the farthest yellows of a sky
picked up in gleams and glimmers on the spoons,
the bird bequeaths the wake of its unimaginable voyage;
bleeding from its razor slit of absence is a hope
that Possibility still breathes in the crevices
of the fixed, the settled and the always.

Light

Ethereal, first of things,
quintessence pure......

(1)

In the many layers of the seen, the visual world
seems as solid, as resistant, as a brick;
yet visibilia, woven of weightless light,
are intactile: the baby plucking at a sunbeam
slanting past his cot sees his fingers dipped
in brightness, his hand italic with radiance,
but harvests nothing from this next-to-nothingness.

Tenuous as empty space, light
makes the air seem pudding-thick, and
smoke indented crags, not plumes, of blue.
Milton's 'ethereal' is too gross; excess baggage
for voyages to the moon inserted in the pause
between one rapid heart-beat and the next,
for unimaginable haste that churns no wake.

(2)

The self-consciousness of space, image
of awareness in the air. But not self-lit:
lacking brightness until the seeing 'I'
kindles to the million-folded complex
of the shining and the seen: glimmers,
assertive glistenings, glitterings and glares,
the rumpled, multi-coloured surfaces of sight.

(3)
Being haunted is the price of being seen -
their caricatures in charcoal at their feet
clutter solid objects in the light.
(A passion almost Prussian for the rules,
an angular precision, rectitude,
sharpens up these outposts of the dark).

Brightness fathers dullness, brilliancies gloom,
and radiance punches blind-spots in the eye.
So darkness, whether blink-sips or whole nights,
is more a complement than opposite of light:
in death the darkness fails along with light.

Milton praised the light with quilled black ink
and made this 'first of things' back into word;
believed God used lampless words to light the void.

Inner Space

I never took those angels by surprise.
However slick the shutters of my eyes,
they'd slip away through cracks they found in space
as if their vanishing were locked by grace
to my intent to catch them out in flight.
They left no after-glow to thin the night,
nor sign to yeast the dullness of my prayers.

Some decades on, I'm through with such affairs,
with chasing wisps of seraphs on the hop,
commuting in their night gowns (God, Non-stop).
I watch the scudding images instead
that set themselves alight when I'm in bed,
the multi-coloured pell-mell of my brain,
the murals that my lids bear like a stain,
the frescoes in the vestibules of sleep
that exercise the mind before its leap.

They're no less strange than cherubs made of hope
and angels with their faces smooth as soap
borrowed from the prints stuck up in school.
I wonder (though incurious as a rule)
what forms these bubbling maverick suds of sight,
these absences tattooed upon the night.

Are images the light the eye once drank
re-lit within the wet-ware's memory bank?
Their brightness in the dark would then make sense:
a candle bleached by noon is less intense,

but glows, a little sun, in lampless night;
and leaves emit a yellow that's more bright
in late October's sun-lorn days of gloom.
As quieter sounds in quietness fill a room
or sudden sneezes shatter Silent Night -
thus mental sights, pale echoes of the light.

Alas for (Scotsman) Hume, the system he proposed
reduced our minds to cisterns filled when hosed,
or buckets lacking handles or a side,
hallways built of whispers, echoes from outside,
in health uncentred as delirium,
sans apperceptive me-continuum.
Herr Kant deduced the image had to be
connected to the other parts of me:
without a self to unify the world,
the cosmos into chaos would be hurled.

Sensations from the bedclothes in the dark,
our knowledge of the past, walks in the park,
must link with moonlit images from dreams,
cohering through the mind's transcendent schemes.
Envisaged thus, the image finds its place,
a prize that awarded to itself by inner space.

O brightness in the dark's remotest sea,
I question these tautologies of me,
this nothing, trawling glints from inner lakes
suspended in a space the 'I' half-makes.

The sceptics give those questions scarce a glance:
"You've brought those angels back to see them dance,
to count them as they shimmy on a pin.
A look at words would show another spin,
revealing 'inner realms' as fakes of thought,
as places extant only in report,
their shadows aren't the substance of what thinks,
but muddles made by language and its kinks."

Dismissed by Oxbridge dons with great disdain,
they seem no more than grammar can explain:
items that are fictions of the mind,
itself a fiction of some higher kind...
But fiction piled on fiction leans on fact -
as shelves are real where paperbacks are packed.
So somewhere fictions end and I begin
For I'm no bloody angel on a pin.
Awake amid the things that come to me
there's something like a self I have to be.

The skull strikes up, sets echo-lights at play,
as self, processing sleepwards, drifts away....
all-seeing, since it *is* the things it 'sees'
and yet it seems to lie outside of these,
though nearer me than anything that's mine.
There's no-one knows just where to draw the line.
I am the thing that makes them, true enough,
and yet they're ready-made, made out of stuff
I've not the slightest notion how to make:
I couldn't make them even by mistake.

A dream's an image swollen to a world:
we lie inside ourselves, a foetus curled.
The dreaming mind glows sun-like in the night,
its sleep a wild unfolding of its flight:
see leaves of day make forests in the dark
and streets unfurl like songs sung by a lark.

What is this sun that warms the dreamed up leaves,
the dancing happiness the sleeper weaves,
the laughter lent to half-forgotten faces,
the eyes that glint at long-forgotten graces?

Elusive as the sound-smoke of a choir,
or an enigmatic girl viewed through desire,
an 'I' pursued by slogan-toting herds,
refusing to be simplified by words -
what are these creatures caged in inner space
and what am I who make and am their place,
who let them uninvited come to me?
Am I the net, the fish, the drowning sea?

The Topiarists of Inlight

...that *active* uncertainty called thinking.
John Dewey

Passive

Silvered surprise
held note of amaze
breve queued on breve
O's out in rows
as in 'shoon of the moon'.
Omicron* of mouth
unpursed to omega;*
inspired awe
smoothly dilating
the stops of the eyes.

Active

Till light at the centre
discovers the dark.
Wonder then wonders
and verbs its amaze.
Radiant thisness becomes
a halo that speaks.
O turns into Oh!
and Oh! into Oh? –
into silvering surprise.

*'Omicron' (little 'o') and 'omega' (big 'o') are letters of the Greek alphabet.

Ambition

Hope thickened time to waiting,
twisted weeks to clenched expectancy that
pregnant years delivered only of promise,
delay, disappointment, spurs, and hardening resolve.

His wife and children ("those I should have loved")
were interruptions, clutter on the path to fame;
ghosts because outside the glamour that
soured his days by staying far away.
"They live their lives, while I am still unborn".
The laughter of his children in the sun
italicised his doomed obscurity,
mocked the vinegar sea he swam across alone.
The rosebay cottage was a catacomb
where his neglected talent lay immured.

His youth ran dry, his marriage died away,
loved ones learned to look elsewhere for love.
He found himself unbothered and alone.

And still the weeks were mildewed cul de sacs
and still the whistling postman stopped his bike
to pluck the world's indifference from his sack,
returning another message he'd addressed
to silence, to the future, to the sky,
and axed away another bottom rung.
"The months are adding up to growing old".
Failure scribbled lines across his face.

At length the long-wooed future turned its gaze.
Degree by slow degree, minute by minute,
his fame's arc rose above the crowd,
assumed a labelled orbit in the world's
collective inattentiveness of mind.
The courted Goddess came to take him in,
cradled his grey head in her cool arms,
fed him scentless adjectives of praise.

Printed words buzzed round his printed thoughts.
Discussed by names who did not know his face,
anthologised and quoted, PhD'd,
he read about himself without delight
and found out who he was in strangers' eyes.

He thought across the things he'd brushed aside:
his youth, of course; his broken, lonely wife;
the childhoods of his children, now far away;
the tender shoots Ambition had laid waste.

Fame and *Festschrift* : ante-rooms of death.
He summarised it all a week before he died:
"Fate smiles at last and Lo! her teeth are black".

IRON Press is among the country's longest established independent literary publishers. The press began operations in 1973 with IRON Magazine which ran for 83 editions until 1997. Since 1975 we have also brought out a regular list of individual collections of poetry, fiction and drama plus various anthologies ranging from *Voices of Conscience, Limerick Nation, The Poetry of Perestroika, 100 Island Poems* and *Cold Iron, Ghost Stories from the 21st Century* and forthcoming, *Trees* (poems) and *Aliens* (fiction).

The press is one of the leading independent publishers of haiku in the UK. Since 2013 we have also run a biennial IRON Press Festival round the harbour in our native Cullercoats. The IRON OR Festival took place in June 2019.

We are delighted to be a part of Inpress Ltd, which was set up by Arts Council England to support independent literary publishers. Go to our website (www.ironpress.co.uk) for full details of our titles and activities.